AN INTRODUCTION TO EARLY
ENGLISH GRAMMAR

Also by the author:

READINGS IN EARLY ENGLISH
LANGUAGE HISTORY

AN INTRODUCTION TO

Early English Grammar

LEONARD H. FREY

San Diego State College

---◆◄◆►◆---

The Odyssey Press · New York

For

Ruth

Margaret

and

Judith

Preface

This study is an attempt at a fairly concise, readable history of English grammar in the first millennium of its development, from the classical Old English period (*c.* 800) to the Elizabethan era. It is *not* a thorough systematic coverage of all aspects of Old, Middle, and early Modern English, but rather a definition of early English largely through its Germanic basis in Old English, and the most emphatic modifications and preservations of that basis. The reader is duly advised to "start at the beginning," with the discussions of the more (Indo-European) and less (Germanic) general backgrounds for English language history.

The reader is also advised that certain important and interesting dimensions of early English are treated briefly or hardly at all. Vocabulary development, though phases of it are suggested in the following chapters, is not accorded its due. And the phonological discussion in chapter three is limited to a number of obvious general considerations.

So much for disclaimers. The author would perhaps be presumptuous to claim with Samuel Johnson that "In this work, when it shall be found that much is omitted, let it not be forgotten that much likewise is performed"; yet, after all, that must in some degree be the hope of anyone offering up another "grammar." If this brief history inspires a few enthusiasts to take a longer look at early English, good enough. If it inspires fewer yet to a *commitment* to early English, better still.

I must thank Mrs. Mary Huntley of San Diego State College for secretarial assistance in the preparation of the manuscript.

Contents

I	Indo-European Background	1
II	Germanic Background	11
III	The Sounds of Early English	23
IV	Noun History	31
V	Pronoun History	43
VI	Verb History	53
VII	Early English Syntax	67
	Appendix	75
	Suggestions for Further Reading	81

AN INTRODUCTION TO EARLY
ENGLISH GRAMMAR

CHAPTER ONE

Indo-European Background

English, at present the most widely spoken of the world's languages, is a member of the Indo-European language community or complex,[1] specifically a Germanic member of that community. An understanding of early English language characteristics and problems depends in good measure on the relationship of English to Indo-European and to Germanic; and therefore a survey of these is in order.

[1] Among the other major language families are the following: Semitic-Hamitic, Finno-Ugric, Malayo-Polynesian, Altaic, Chinese-Burmese-Tibetan, Japanese-Korean, as well as the numerous groupings of African, Australian, and American Indian languages.

1

I

Indo-European[2] is the name generally given a very considerable group of languages spoken by as much as half the world's population and ranging world-wide geographically. The term itself is useful in defining a profile for the extension of the group from the Asian subcontinent of India in the east to Europe and the spheres of European influence in the west. The stating and clarifying of this profile may be called the beginning of the modern science of linguistics in general.

In 1786 Sir William Jones, a British jurist in India, suggested certain basic similarities between Sanskrit, the ancient Indian ritual dialect, and the classical European languages, Greek and Latin, as well as English. Resemblances among many of the European languages had previously been recognized, but in effect here for the first time was a linking of languages of very divergent cultures, continents apart. The nineteenth century saw the study and classification of a large number of European and Asian languages and the establishment of a remarkable community of relationships. Today, there is essential agreement about the branches and members of the Indo-European family, although defining terms may differ somewhat. For convenience, Indo-European scholarship speaks of a *satem*, or eastern, and a *centum*, or western, grouping of the member branches.[3] Indic, Iranian, Armenian, Albanian, and Balto-

---

[2] Or Indo-Germanic, a term sometimes employed by European (especially Germanic) scholars.

[3] *Satem* and *centum* are the Persian and Latin terms for the concept "hundred" and are convenient cognates for geographical grouping.

Slavic are *satem* languages; Hellenic, Italic, Celtic, and Germanic are *centum* languages.

Indic includes Sanskrit, the Prakrits, and their descendants. Sankrit means "correct, regulated" and refers to the language of ancient scripture, the Vedas and Upanishads, and the national epics (the *Ramayana* and *Mahabharata*). The Vedic texts (*c.* 1500 B.C.) represent perhaps the earliest examples and Panini's Sanskrit grammar (fourth century B.C.) the earliest study of an Indo-European language.[4] Sanskrit survives today purely in literary and ritual usage; the spoken languages of India derive from the Prakrits, of which an early example, Pali, is the language of the Buddhist canon. Hindi and Urdu are important as the official languages of India and Pakistan, and Bengali, Punjabi and Romany (the Gypsy dialect) are among the better-known Indic dialects. Sanskrit is considered one of the most important languages of the Indo-European family for the archaic linguistic evidence it offers, e.g., eight cases for the noun.

Iranian, too, involves a literary-ritualistic dialect, Avestan, and a spoken one, Persian. The former is the language of the Zoroastrian religion, the latter the source of numerous modern dialects, including Kurdish and Afghan. The modern Persian vocabulary has been generally influenced by Semitic Arabic. Old Persian inscribed in cuneiform characters in a tri-lingual memorial to the emperor Darius provided the key to the decipherment of the very ancient languages of Mesopotamia.

[4] The Greek writings of *Linear B* deciphered by Michael Ventris and the Hittite cuneiform tablets from Boghazkoy in Anatolia are very possibly older.

Armenian, considered by some to be a relative of the Phrygian conceivably spoken by Homer's Trojans, was long rated a branch of Iranian but now occupies an independent position, due to certain unusual consonantal features.

Albanian, like Armenian, shows considerable foreign influence, especially Greek, Turkish, and Slavic. The written records for the language begin rather late, in the fourteenth century A.D.; behind them may be the ancient Illyrian.

Balto-Slavic is classified in two groups. Of the Baltic languages Prussian[5] is some three centuries extinct, while Latvian and Lithuanian remain in usage. Lithuanian, a most conservative language, preserves features of pitch and inflection more similar to Sanskrit than to many of its modern relatives. Accordingly, it is of primary interest to Indo-Europeanists and is studied as an important link with the community's past. The Slavic languages are usually discussed geographically: Russian and Ukrainian constitute the Eastern, Polish and Czech the Western, and Bulgarian, Serbo-Croatian, and Slovenian the Southern branches. Old Bulgarian, or Old Church Slavonic, is preserved in religious texts, the oldest records for the Slavic group (ninth century A.D.). There are a general archaism and similarity among members of this group, more so than in western groupings like the Germanic or Romance.

The *Hellenic* dialects are Aeolic, Doric, and Ionic. Doric was the language of the Spartan victors over the Ionic-speaking Athenians; yet Ionic, the language of the Aegean

---

[5] Terms like *Prussian* and *Saxon* as used for linguistic definition may have little or no relation to ideas or places generally associated with them.

islands (Homer), and later the *Koine* of the eastern Mediterranean world, provided the basis for modern spoken Greek. As the medium for the ancient Athenian cultural achievement, Attic Ionic is obviously one of the great languages of western civilization.

Of the *Italic* dialects, Umbrian and Oscan once coexisted with Latin as the languages of northern and southern Italy. The spread of Latin from its beginnings at Latium on the Tiber is bound up with the vast history of Roman culture in general. The spoken "vulgar" rather than the literary language[6] was carried by soldiers and merchants into the colonies of the empire and became the basis for the Romance grouping of today. Spanish, Catalan, and Portuguese may be considered a subgrouping, as may French and Provençal. The latter was important in medieval culture as the language of the southern French troubadours and the courtly love literature. Italian represents the continuous development of Latin as spoken in the city of Rome itself. Rumanian, as might be expected, shows Slavic influence in its vocabulary. Romanic, or Romansch, is a dialect of northeast Italy and Switzerland. Spanish, Portuguese, and French made their way west and east in the centuries of maritime imperialism, and today they are widely spoken in both the New World and the Orient.

The history of the *Celtic* languages is one of decline from wide usage in western Europe in pre-Christian times to a precarious existence in the British Isles and northern

---

[6] *Caballus* and *equus* aptly represent the difference between the vulgar and classical Latin. From the former, the Romance group derives such horse-concepts as *caballero* and *chevalier;* from the latter English gets the formal term *equestrian.*

France today. The ancient Gauls carried their speech to Britain, where two Celtic branches developed: Gaelic (Irish, Scottish, and Manx) and Britannic (Welsh and Cornish). Of these, Cornish is nearly two centuries extinct, while all others are losing ground before English. Despite such efforts as Irish nationalism to preserve the Gaelic tongue, it is likely that Celtic in the British Isles will in the future be entirely displaced. A Britannic relative, Breton, survives today in Brittany, whence it was borne by Celtic fugitives from the Anglo-Saxon conquerors of England.

The *Germanic* group, of primary importance for us as speakers of English, is generally classified as Eastern, Northern, and Western. Eastern Germanic is limited to Gothic, the oldest recorded language in the group. From the fourth century A.D. survive portions of Bishop Wulfila's translation of the Bible from Greek. These Gothic texts are obviously literary and regularized but they suggest something of the possible nature of proto-Germanic. Northern Germanic means the Scandinavian languages, for which Norse-Icelandic and Swedish-Danish constitute subgroups. The conservative Icelandic was in medieval times the medium of a highly developed literature, the sagas and the eddas, the latter our best source for common Germanic mythology. Western Germanic divides into "High" and "Low," which terms pertain to geography, the mountainous terrain of southern Germany and the northern coastal plain respectively. High German developed as the language of Germany today, while Low German consisted of Saxon (modern Plattdeutsch), Franconian (modern Dutch and Flemish), Frisian, and "English."

Old English and Anglo-Saxon are interchangeable terms,

the first useful in suggesting a continuity from the Germanic settlement of England to the present, the second specifying two of the Germanic tribes invading the island.[7] The Germanic languages in general and High German in particular are characterized by a shifting of certain consonants away from the common Indo-European pattern. More will be said of this and other Germanic matters in the following chapter.

In addition to these nine branches of Indo-European, two languages have in the past half century been added to the complex: Tocharian and Hittite. The former, from Chinese Turkestan, is as yet little understood, although it oddly appears to share certain characteristics with the western *centum* rather than the eastern *satem* group. Hittite, on the other hand, has become a focal point in Indo-European studies. Some maintain that this Anatolian language may stand coequal to Indo-European rather than as one of its offshoots, thus suggesting Indo-Hittite as a redefining term for the complex.

II

Whether Indo-European is defined as nine, ten, or eleven branches, it would seem obvious that behind the profile of *satem-centum* relationships there stands a hypothetical parent language from which the member branches diverged in some pattern of migration, presumably a pattern developing over millennia. Obvious, too, the absence of Proto-Indo-European records as such. The entire Indo-

[7] The reader will find both terms used, quite indiscriminately, in this book.

European thesis has been one of reconstruction from the most archaic and conservative evidence in the branches themselves, e.g., similarities between Sanskrit and Lithuanian, such as cognate relationships among words for certain common concepts. Compare the following vocabulary for *mother* and *three*:

mātr	SANSKRIT	tri
mair	ARMENIAN	erek
matj	RUSSIAN	tri
motina	LITHUANIAN	tris
matēr	GREEK	treīs
māter	LATIN	trēs
mama	RUMANIAN	trei
mãe	PORTUGUESE	tres
mathair	IRISH	tri
moðir	ICELANDIC	þrja
moeder	DUTCH	drie
mutter	GERMAN	drei

Only the Armenian *erek* falls outside the cognate patterns here. The M-T-R and T-R consonantal clusters for the two concepts prevail to a remarkable degree. Paul Thieme has offered a graphic hypothetical reconstruction of Indo-European on the basis of *God has given teeth; God will give bread*. The Latin *Deus dedit dentes; Deus dabit et panem* and the Lithuanian *Dievas dawe dantis; Dievas duos ir duonos* might together suggest the Indo-European *Deivos ededot dntns; Deivos dedot dhonas.*[8]

[8] Cf. "The Indo-European Language," *Scientific American*, vol. 199 (Oct. 1958), p. 74.

The location of the original Indo-European community has been a topic of interesting if inconclusive speculation. Early in the nineteenth century scholarship favored the Near East, with its aura of Biblical beginnings, "the confusion of tongues" at Babel, and the evidence of Indo-European Indic and Iranian contiguous to the area. The more recent suggestion of north central Europe was largely on the strength of vocabulary evidence. Many of the Indo-European languages have cognates for *oak, pine, bear, wolf, beaver, rabbit, tortoise, bee, owl, snow,* and *winter* but no cognates for concepts peculiar to a torrid or tropical zone. Similarly, the root *laks,* which in Balto-Slavic and German (*lachs*)[9] denotes *salmon,* in Iranian *trout,* and in Tocharian *fish,* suggests the possible pattern of Indo-European migration. The salmon is native to north central Europe, including the Baltic area, whence the root *laks* may have been carried eastward and been transferred, first to the trout as the ranking fish of the Iranian plateau, then to the generalized concept of fish, in the easternmost thrust of the migration, in Chinese Turkestan. Additionally, the Sanskrit *laksha* and *lākshā* refer to *great amount* and *reddish-pink resin,* respectively. Conceivably, these concepts may originate in salmon-shoal and salmon-color, as the Indic peoples originally knew them.[10]

According to this locating of the original Indo-European complex, the Baltic Lithuanians may represent the non-migratory element and reflect this in their language. It must be added, however, that the emergence of Hittite as

[9] As with the kosher delicatessen favorite, *lox.*
[10] Thieme, op. cit., p. 73.

part of the complex has suggested for some a location nearer the Caucasus. The transition from neolithic to bronze cultures in the third millennium B.C. is the generally favored chronology for the dispersal of the speculated Indo-European community.

CHAPTER TWO

Germanic Background

The history of the English language begins with the Germanic invasions of Britain in the fifth century A.D. For about a thousand years prior to this time, Britain was a Celtic language area, with considerable Roman cultural influence from the first century A.D. The earlier history of Britain is obscure: pre-Celtic monuments like Stonehenge may be the work of a Mediterranean race that migrated north in the neolithic era.[1]

The British Celtics stoutly resisted Julius Caesar's efforts in the first century B.C., and it was only a century later that the Roman legions under Agricola made England

[1] The "Iberian" stage of British history has yielded no written records as such.

an outpost of the Empire. Evidence of Roman stonecraft in roads and buildings remains from the centuries of occupation, as do numerous Latin inscriptions, which suggest that the Celtic aristocracy, at least, took up the Roman *mores* and cultivated the Roman *pax*. By the early fifth century, Rome was sufficiently pressured on the continent to withdraw from the island, and for a generation the Celts wallowed in unprofitable feuds with the Scottish Picts, northerners who had resisted the civilizing ways of Rome and retained the earlier barbaric ruggedness in warfare. Finally, in 449 according to Bede, the south Celtic chieftain Vortigern enlisted German mercenary aid in the feuds. The *Anglo-Saxon Chronicle* gives a vivid account of this turning point in British history:

Year 449. At this time Martin and Valentine assumed rule and reigned seven winters. And in their days Hengest and Horsa, invited by Vortigern, the British king, came to Britain at that place that is called Ebbsfleet, at first as help to the British, but afterwards they fought against them.

The king ordered them to fight against the Picts, and they did so, and had victory wherever they came. Then they sent to Anglia, and ordered them to send more troops; and they ordered them to declare the worthlessness of the British and the choiceness of the land. They then sent them more troops. Then men came from three German nations: from the Old Saxons, from the Angles, from the Jutes.

From the Jutes came the people of Kent and the people of Wight—that is the nation that now lives on Wight—and that tribe among the West Saxons that one still calls the "tribe of Jutes." From the Old Saxons came the East Saxons and South Saxons and West Saxons. From Anglia—which ever since stood waste between the Jutes and Saxons—came the East Angles, Middle Angles, Mercians, and all the Northumbrians.

The Jutes, from that part of continental Denmark called Schleswig-Holstein today, apparently formed the vanguard of the invasion; but it was the more numerous Angles and Saxons that dominated in the Germanic settlement of England. The Angles, from the coastal plain between Jutland and the Elbe River, established themselves in the northern and eastern area of the island and gave the island and language their name. The Saxons, from the plain between the Elbe and the Netherlands, settled in the south and west.[2]

It is traditional to assume common bonds and interests as well as language among these Germanic tribes, and this is doubtless true in the main. But archaeology has offered interesting dissimilarities as well, e.g., cremation among the Angles but not among the Saxons or Jutes. It is reasonable to suppose that the three peoples arrived at a political-military forbearance among themselves that was reflected in the "Heptarchy" or seven-kingdom structure of England between the sixth and eleventh centuries.[3]

The Anglian kingdoms of Northumbria and Mercia held the balance of power in the seventh and eighth centuries, respectively. Northumbria was the seat of monastic culture, and most of the important Old English poetry was written there, along with Bede's history. Alcuin, a product

[2] The continental homes of the three tribes have been disputed, e.g., a Frankish origin has been claimed for the Jutes.

[3] Northumbria, Mercia, East Anglia (Anglian); Essex, Sussex, Wessex (Saxon); Kent (Jutish).

of the cathedral school at York, became Northumbria's greatest contribution to the intellectual life of continental Europe as the educational supervisor of Charlemagne's Frankish court.[4]

From eighth century Mercia survive many of the charters and laws that form a basis for English common law. The Mercian kingdom was to assume its greatest prominence in the Middle English period as the Midland area that developed the modern standard English language.

The close of the eighth century saw the beginning of the Danish Viking incursions on England, at first in the north and east, then in the ensuing two centuries increasingly inland. The Saxon kingdom of Wessex emerged as the leader in this intra-Germanic struggle; and for the remainder of the pre-Conquest period Wessex was the center of English political and cultural life. The West Saxon leader Alfred (871–899) was the first great English king, distinguished for his resistance to the Danes, his conservation of Northumbrian learning, and his sense of an English identity and purpose. In his preface to the *Pastoral Care*, he writes of England's past and his hopes for preserving it:

. . . it has very often come into my mind what wise men there formerly were throughout England, both of sacred and secular orders; and what happy times there were then throughout England; and how the kings who had power over the nation in those days obeyed God and His ministers; how they preserved peace,

---

[4] The Celtic monastic influence on Old English culture forms a fascinating chapter in early English history, as does Alcuin's famous criticism of the monks of Lindisfarne ("Quis Inieldus cum Christo?"), which suggests the possibility of a considerable monastic knowledge of Germanic folk-culture and history.

morality, and order at home, and at the same time enlarged their territory abroad; and how they prospered both with war and with wisdom . . . Therefore it seems better to me . . . for us also to translate some books which are most needful for all men to know into the language which we can all understand, and for you to do as we very easily can if we have tranquillity enough, that is, that all the youth now in England of free men, who are rich enough to be able to devote themselves to it, be set to learn as long as they are not fit for any other occupation, until they are able to read English writing well; and let those be afterwards taught more in the Latin language who are to continue in learning, and be promoted to a higher rank.[5]

The Danes were to increase their strength and authority in England to the point where in the generation preceding the Norman conquest the Danish Cnut actually reigned as the English king. The Germanic settlement of the island, then, occurred in two stages: first came the displacement of the Celts by the Anglo-Saxon group, then the temporary domination of the English by the Scandinavians. Linguistically, the latter is mainly of importance in the area of vocabulary, most notably in the Scandinavian contribution to the English pronoun.[6]

I

When we consider some of the specifically Germanic features of the English language, we might well begin with the famous phonological description known as Grimm's Law. In 1822 Jacob Grimm, of the folklore brothers Grimm, offered a set of consonant correspondences which explained

[5] Cook, A. S. and Tinker, C. B., eds., *Select Translations from Old English Prose*, Cambridge: Harvard Univ. Press, 1936, pp. 101–103.

[6] The pronouns *they, their, them* enter English from Scandinavian.

certain regular differences between cognates in the Germanic languages and the other Indo-European languages. Nine consonants in each grouping are involved. The following chart offers cognate examples from the Modern English vocabulary where possible, relying on derivatives from the Indo-European Greek or Latin to match the Germanic English:[7]

1. Indo-European *p* corresponds with Germanic *f*. Examples: *p*edestrian/*f*oot, *p*aternal/*f*atherly, *p*utrid/*f*oul, *p*ecuniary/*f*ee, *p*en/*f*eather.

2. Indo-European *t* corresponds with Germanic *th*. Examples: *t*riangle/*th*ree, *t*enuous/*th*in, *t*orrid/*th*irst, ma*t*ernal/mo*th*erly, den*t*ist/too*th*.

3. Indo-European *k* corresponds with Germanic *h*. Examples: *c*ornet/*h*orn, *c*anine/*h*ound, *c*ordial/*h*earty, capi*t*al/*h*ead, *c*entury/*h*undred.

4. Indo-European *b* corresponds with Germanic *p*. Examples: lu*b*ricate/sli*pp*ery, *b*ursar/*p*urse, du*b*us (Lithuanian)/dee*p*, tro*b*a (Bulgarian)/thor*p*, sla*b*u (Slavic)/slee*p*.

5. Indo-European *d* corresponds with Germanic *t*. Examples: *d*ecimal/*t*en, *d*ual/*t*wo, *d*entist/*t*ooth, e*d*ible/ea*t*, *d*ocile/*t*each.

6. Indo-European *g* corresponds with Germanic *k*. Examples:*g*rain/*c*orn, a*g*riculture/a*c*re, *g*enus/*k*in, *g*elid/*c*old, *g*enuflect/*k*nee.

---

[7] Generally Latin and Greek yield obvious cognate material. Occasionally in the examples cited a less familiar Indo-European language is the provider.

7. Indo-European *bh*[8] corresponds with Germanic *b* Examples: *bh*ārati (Sanskrit)/*f*erry/*b*ear, *bh*rātr (Sanskrit)/*f*raternal/*b*rother.

8. Indo-European *dh* corresponds with Germanic *d*. Examples: mā*dh*u (Sanskrit)/mea*d*.

9. Indo-European *gh*[8] corresponds with Germanic *g*. Examples: *h*ostile/*g*uest, *h*orticulture/*g*arden.

How, or why, this Germanic departure from Indo-European took place, scholarship is unprepared to say. The dating of the change is also highly uncertain; sometime late in the first millennium B.C. is the general assumption. What we can be sure of is that these correspondences hold with impressive regularity and where irregularities occur, the theorem known as Verner's Law explains them.[9] A second consonant shift affects High German and separates it from the common Germanic; thus High German develops a *t* for the Germanic *d* (English *d*eep, *d*eer/High German *t*ief, *T*ier); a *pf* for the Germanic *p* (English *p*ipe, stum*p*/High German *pf*eife, Stum*pf*); and a *z* for the Germanic *t* (English *t*ooth, *t*en/High German *Z*ahn, *z*ehn). English and modern Dutch thus share consonants that have shifted in the modern High German.

If the English vocabulary originally qualifies as a part of the Germanic linguistic complex, it has in its millennium

---

[8] The Indo-European *bh* of the Sanskrit became *f* in Latin; Indo-European *gh* became Latin *h*.

[9] Karl Verner clarified certain exceptions to Grimm's Law by noting the effect of accentuation in Germanic language development. Thus, unlike Indo-European in general, Germanic word families show a regular stress on the root-syllable: *king, kingly, kingship, kingdom* (cf. Latin *family, familiar, familiarity*).

and a half of history become so receptive to borrowing from other Indo-European and non-Indo-European languages as to be the most cosmopolitan vocabulary on earth. (By contrast, the Germanic Icelandic word-stock has remained quite conservative and is today the best living repository for the Germanic roots in their older forms.) It should be noted, however, that much of the heavy-duty vocabulary of modern English—the auxiliary verbs, familial terms, and the numerals are obvious examples—is Germanic; and a modern English speaker could doubtless make do very intelligibly on a diet of Germanic English vocabulary.

II

In discussing grammar, a twofold distinction must be made. Those European grammatical systems with a fairly heavy degree of inflection, or change in word-form, are termed *synthetic;* those with less stress on inflection are termed *analytic.* Greek, Latin, German, Russian, and Old English would be numbered among the former; the Romance languages and Modern English among the latter. The differing emphasis on inflection may lead to strikingly different conceptual contrasts between grammars, as Baugh points out for Latin and Modern English.[10] For Latin, with its methodical inflection of nouns, a sentence like "Nero Agrippinam interfecit" can only mean "Nero killed Agrippina," no matter what the order of the words. For the sentence to mean anything else, the nominative (subject) form of Nero would have to be inflected and the accusative (object) form of Agrippinam would have to be changed. For

[10] In *A History of the English Language,* 2nd ed., New York: Appleton-Century-Crofts, 1957, p. 64.

Modern English on the other hand, with its near lack of inflection for nouns, the positioning of the terms is all-important: "Agrippina killed Nero" is the opposite of "Nero killed Agrippina." To choose a slightly more complicated illustration from Latin: "Acrisius volebat Perseum nepotem suum necare" can only mean "Acrisius wished to kill his grandson Perseus," no matter what the stylistic ordering of the syntax. "Perseum nepotem suum" is a masculine accusative phrase, "Acrisius" a masculine nominative form, "volebat" a past tense singular third person form, and "necare" an infinitive; no other interpretation is possible here. To reverse the subject and object of the action of the verb phrase, we must render "Perseus nepos suus" and "Acrisium." Then, whether or not "Perseus" precedes or follows "Acrisium" is immaterial; word-form has absolutely determined sentence meaning.

Old English or Anglo-Saxon, though somewhat less heavily inflected than Latin, shares with the latter an essential determination of sentence meaning through word-form rather than position. The rather complex syntax of the opening of *Beowulf* may illustrate this:

> Hwæt, wē Gār-Dena in gēardagum,
> þēodcyninga þrym gefrūnon,
> hūþā æþelingas ellen fremedon!

Taking the word order quite literally here, this may be rendered "What, we of Spear-Danes in yore-days of people-kings valor learned; how the nobles bravery did." It is from the inflections that we establish something like an idiomatic statement. "Gār-Dena," a genitive plural, modifies "þēod-cyninga," another genitive plural, which in turn modifies the accusative singular "þrym." The pronoun "wē," a nominative plural, is the subject of the past first person plural "gefrūnon," the verb for the first clause, which thus may be read "Lo, we have learned of the valor of the tribal-kings of the Spear-Danes in former times." The second clause is more straightforward: the only inversion here is that of the accusative singular "ellen" and the past third person plural "fremedon," thus, "how the nobles did brave things." In Old English poetry, where alliterative sound patterns dominate, the high degree of inflection allows for very free syntactic patterns to accommodate the alliteration.

The degree of inflection in a language may largely determine the flexibility of its syntax, yet much Old English prose yields word-order very close to the modern English. Consider the following, from the Old English version of the St. Matthew Gospel (20: 8–10), translated from the Latin of St. Jerome:

> Sōþlīce þā hit wæs ǣfen geworden, þā sægde se wīngeardes hlāford his gerēfan: "Clipa þā wyrhtan, and āgief him hiera mēde; onginn fram þǣm ȳtemestan oþ þone fyrmestan." Eornostlīce þā þā gecōmon þe ymbe þā endleoftan tīd cōmon, þā onfēngon hīe ǣlc his pening. And þā þe þǣr ǣrest cōmon wēndon þæt hīe scolden māre onfōn; þā onfēngon hīe syndrige peningas.

(A literal rendering of this: Truly, when it was evening become, then said the vineyard's lord to his reeve: "Call the workers and give them their reward; begin from the outmost unto the foremost." Indeed, when they came who about the eleventh hour came, then received they each his penny. And they that there first came thought they should more receive; then received they separate pennies.) The word-order here, apart from subject-verb inversions and simplified past tense, is essentially that of Modern English.

For synthetic grammars like Old English, as for analytic grammars like Modern English, the primary parts of speech are the nouns, pronouns, and verbs. From these and these alone independent clauses may be made and maintained. The history of early English grammar is largely the history of these parts of speech. The very complex and elaborate system of auxiliary constructions that underlies Modern English syntax must be understood against the background of early English noun, pronoun, and verb history. The levelling of inflection from Old through Middle to Modern English shifted the grammatical emphasis so that determination of meaning now depends not on word-form but on word-position. Accordingly, it is the noun, the pronoun, and the verb that will mainly occupy us in the subsequent chapters. Each of these parts of speech warrants separate treatment according to the grammatical aspects pertaining to it. But before we inquire into these, we should note the rudimentary sound-patterns of earlier English.

CHAPTER THREE

The Sounds of Early English

The literature on the phonetics and phonology of early English is vast and erudite,[1] a recognition of the complex nature of sound-structure and sound-change, particularly in the Germanic stage of English language development and in the creation (in late Middle and early Modern English) of the sounds of the language we know today. It is our purpose here to do no more than brief the student on the sounds of early English, first through the rationale of pronunciation for Old English, Middle English, and early Modern English and second through a short survey of

[1] Cf. J. and E. M. Wright, *Old English Grammar* and *An Elementary Middle English Grammar;* H. Kökeritz, *Shakespeare's Pronunciation,* for a start.

sound-change for the language from *c.* 800–1600. No more than a most superficial statement will be attempted concerning the relationship of the sounds of Old English to those of its Germanic parent or siblings; this relationship is the concern of comparative Germanic phonology and is in itself a highly problematic area.

I

It is common knowledge that Modern English spelling is almost spectacularly difficult in the relationship of sound and symbol. George Bernard Shaw left a small fortune he wanted employed in a reform attempt for English spelling, noting that according to our present spelling possibilities "ghoti" should be a perfectly possible spelling for "fish."[2] In contrast, modern German spelling is extremely reliable; the relationships among sound, symbol, and syllabics are consistent and coherent. In a sense, the history of English spelling is the story of good gone bad, of a reliable and phonetic spelling in the Germanic phase of English language history that becomes an anachronism as English sounds part company from their European counterparts. A very considerable complicating factor here is the "Great Vowel Shift" of the fifteenth and sixteenth centuries, which makes mavericks of the long vowel qualities of English and leaves them intact as a unique vowel-group in the Indo-European family.[3] It is in the vowels rather than in the consonants that the more radical changes in English language sound have occurred; accordingly, we begin our survey with them.

[2] Skeptics might consider *enough* and *negotiate*.
[3] We will examine this later.

The student of Greek or Latin, of French, Spanish, or German is accustomed to long vowel sounds often designated "continental" and arranged in a sequence from "front" to "back" according to the position of the sound in the mouth. If we use the long mark, or *macron*, to indicate the long vowel sound, these continental vowels, from front to back, are *ī* (equivalent to Modern English b*ee*), *ē* (equivalent to Modern English h*a*te), *ā* (equivalent to Modern English f*a*ther), *ō* (equivalent to Modern English b*oa*t), and *ū* (equivalent to Modern English t*oo*th). The Modern English examples are not capricious; they should indicate the problem inherent in our spelling. The *Beowulf*-poet of the eighth century, or Chaucer six centuries later, would have rhymed *bee* with our Modern English *may*, *hate* with *got*, *boat* with *hot*, and *tooth* with *sloth;* only *father* would have sounded familiar. The following Old and Middle English forms will illustrate the continental vowel qualities operative in English until the early Modern stage:

	Old English	*Middle English*	*Modern English*
ī	rīdan	rīden	ride
	þīn	thī	thy
	gelīc	lijc[4]	like
ē	hē	hē	he
	mēd	mēde	meed
	sēon	seen[4]	see
ā	stān	stāne	stone
	hām	hām	home
	nān	nān	none

[4] The Middle English may use *ij* as the equivalent of *ī*, also *ee* for *ē*, *ou* for *ū*.

Old English	Middle English	Modern English
ō	gōd	gōd	good
	brōþor	brōther	brother
	sōþ	sōth	sooth
ū	hūs	hous[4]	house
	dūn	doun[4]	down (n.)
	nū	nou[4]	now

It will be noted that there is a uniform relationship between the continental and Modern English qualities for *ī*, *ē*, and *ū*.[4] The Modern English equivalent for the *ī* is the diphthong *ai*; the equivalent for *ē* is the continental *ī*; the equivalent for *ū* is the diphthong *au*. We may generalize as follows: in Modern English the continental vowel qualities have in most instances been raised (*ē* to *ī*, *ā* to *ē*, *ō* to *ū*) where possible and the extreme front and back qualities (*ī* and *ū*) have been diphthongized. (Thus *fāme*, *fame*, *nāme*, *name*, *rōt*, *root*, *sōt*, *soot*, along with the above.) This shift in vowel qualities was nearly complete by Shakespeare's time, although there is reason to believe that in Elizabethan English the old and new may have for a time coexisted (the vowel in *my*, for example, may have been sounded either as *ī* or as the present diphthong); and we know from Pope's rhyming *obey* and *tea* in "The Rape of the Lock" that in certain instances the *ī-ē* relationship was not entirely settled as late as the eighteenth century.

In addition to the above long vowels, Old English dis-

---

[4] The Middle English may use *ij* as the equivalent of *ī*, also *ee* for *ē*, *ou* for *ū*.

closes a digraph $\bar{æ}$ which is sounded like the vowel in Modern English *hat*. Its appearance is very common in Old English; in Middle English it loses its identity in the $\bar{e}$ which in turn becomes $\bar{\imath}$. Thus Old English $\bar{æ}lc$ (each), $s\bar{æ}d$ (seed), $d\bar{æ}l$ (deal), $m\bar{æ}l$ (meal), $\bar{æ}gþer$ (either).

The Old English consonants fall into two groups, the first familiar and largely unproblematical in that the sounds have much the same value as in Modern English orthography. *B*, *d*, *l*, *m*, *n*, *p*, *t*, *w*, and *x* (spelled *ks*) would qualify here. The second group needs consideration in that a variety of sounds or spellings attaches to them. *C* and *g* are perhaps the most difficult, for each has two common and quite separate soundings. *C* may be pronounced as a velar *K*, as in *candel* (candle), $c\bar{o}l$ (cool), *cuman* (come), *cweþan* (quoth), *cnapa* (boy, knave), *cyning* (king); or it may be pronounced as a palatal *CH*, as in $c\bar{e}osan$ (choose), *cild* (child), *ece* (eternal), *ecg* (edge), *micel* (much), *rice* (kingdom, *Reich*). *G* may be pronounced as a velar *G*, as in $g\bar{a}n$ (go), $g\bar{o}d$ (good), *gadrian* (gather), $g\bar{u}þ$ (battle), *gamen* (sport, game), $g\bar{a}r$ (spear); or it may be pronounced as a palatal *Y*, as in *regen* (rain), $g\bar{e}$ (you, ye), *geard* (yard), *giefu* (gift), *geong* (young), *dæg* (day).

The velar or palatal quality of the sound for both consonants may generally be determined from the proximate vowel. If it is a long or short back vowel (*a*, *o*, *u*: *candel*, *cuman*, *gadrian*, $g\bar{a}r$), the consonant will be hard. If it is a long or short front vowel (*i*, *e*, *æ*: *cild*, *micel*, $g\bar{e}$, *dæg*), the consonant will be soft. If the consonants are followed by the nasal *n* or the liquids *l* or *r*, the consonant will be hard: *cniht* (youth), $cn\bar{e}ow$ (knee), *clipian* (speak, call), $cl\bar{a}þ$

(cloth), *cræft* (power, craft), *cringan* (yield, fall); *gnorn* (sad), *gnidan* (rub, knead), *glidan* (glide), *glæm* (gleam), *gretan* (greet), *gryre* (terror). It must seem obvious from the Chaucerian forms *child*, *chesen*, *muche(l)*, *rich* that Middle English developed a *CH* spelling for the palatal sounding of *C*. It is interesting to note, however, that early Northern English regularly favored the velar sounding where we would expect the palatal, hence, Scots *kirk*.

Middle English spelling took steps to solve the *g* dilemma with a letter called *yogh* and written ȝ. Yogh designated the palatal *g* (ȝung) and additionally the velar *gh* (liȝtliche). The fourteenth century poet of *Gawain and the Green Knight* makes further use of the letter for the *Z* sound, as in *watȝ* (was), *askeȝ* (ashes), *Ȝeferus* (Zephyr). Eventually yogh gave way to *y*, *w*, and *gh* in spelling.

Old English and certain conservative forms of Middle English employ the runic *thorn* (þ) and *eth* (ð) for *th*. Originally the thorn represented the voiceless (as in our *thin*) and the eth the voiced (as in our *those*) sounds, but for practical purposes the two letters became virtually interchangeable. By the fourteenth century the *th* spelling had prevailed in the East Midland dialect (the ancestor of Modern standard English), but at this time West Midland writers like Langland (*Piers Plowman*) and the *Gawain*-poet still employed the thorn.

II

It is noteworthy that in regard to inflection and pronunciation Middle English, as the transitional state of the language, relates to the earlier and later stages of English in almost precisely opposite ways. By Chaucer's time the language had vastly simplified its inflections; the late

Middle English noun, pronoun, and verb are certainly closer to Modern English forms than to Old English or modern German. The final unstressed *-e* that proves something of a puzzle to students learning proper scansion of Chaucer actually represents the levelling of a number of Old English inflections, such as *-a, -u, -an, -en, -on, -um*. Chaucerian morphology, compared with Old English morphology, is quite easily mastered. On the other hand, the sounds of fourteenth century English generally stand in much closer relationship to those of the Old English of a half millennium earlier than to those of the late sixteenth century. A literate fourteenth century Englishman would have had little trouble *reading* Elizabethan literature but he would have found some of its sounds very strange indeed. Any student of English language history needs to appreciate this point. At the same time, the dramatic surge away from the mainstream of Indo-European vocalics represented by the Great Vowel Shift should not obscure the fact that in the Old English stage of the language a number of sound-changes were taking place and were continued into Middle English. These may be briefly accounted for here (1) quantitatively and (2) qualitatively.

(1) The lengthening of short vowels before certain consonant groups: *-ld* (hence Old English *feld* and Modern English *field*; Old English *wilde* and Modern English *wild*), *-mb* (hence Old English *climban* and Modern English *climb*), *-ng* (hence Old English *clingan* and Modern English *cling*; Old English *swingan* and Modern English *swing*).

(2) The altering of certain Old English vowels and diphthongs in Middle English, some of which follow: Old

English *a* to *o* before a nasal in West Midland (hence *mon* in Gawain, *man* in Chaucer), Old English *ā* to *ō* in all dialects except Northern (hence *lord* and Scots *laird*, *ghost* and Scots *gast*, *home* and Scots *hame*), Old English *ea* to *ae* by the end of the Old English period (hence Old English *eald*, Middle English *eld*, Modern English *old*; Old English *weald*, Middle English *wald*, Modern English [Cots]*wolds*), Old English *eo* to *e* during the twelfth century (hence Old English *heord*, Middle English *herde*, Modern English *herd*; Old English *eorre*, Middle English *erre*, Modern English *err*; Old English *eorl*, Middle English *erl*, Modern English *earl*), Old English *ēa* to *ǣ* by the end of the Old English period (hence Old English *dēad*, Middle English *dēde*, Modern English *dead*; Old English *hēafod*, Middle English *hēved*, Modern English *head*)[5], Old English *ēo* to *ē* in the twelfth century (hence Old English *dēop*, Middle English *dēpe*, Modern English *deep*; Old English *hrēocan*, Middle English *rēke*, Modern English *reek*).

The foregoing are no more than a sampling of sound changes that pertain for Old English and Middle English, and that have survived in modern speech. The student of Germanic philology will recognize that for reasons not entirely clear this early stage of English shows a remarkable flexibility in certain vowel patterns. The Great Vowel Shift of the transition from Middle to Modern English is more dramatic, yet the signs of vowel change to come are already present in Germanic English.

[5] In early English phonology, intervocalic *f* becomes *v*, then drops out.

CHAPTER FOUR

Noun History

The student addressing himself to a synthetic grammar like Latin or German for the first time generally finds the noun his chief problem. Granting the extreme formal complexity of the verb in a language like Latin (where the complete conjugation of a single verb may yield upwards of two hundred forms), it is the noun, with its aspects of case, number, and gender, that is the puzzle. The reason for this is simple. The Modern English verb, though its inflections are far fewer than those of the Latin verb, is still a complicated part of speech, what with the numerous auxiliary possibilities designating tense, mood, and voice, and with the adverbial appendages that condition or particularize meaning (*put up with*, *put down*, *put in* may very reasonably be considered verb-ideas, rather than verbs with modifiers).

The Modern English noun, on the other hand, represents a vast simplification of formal, aspectual possibilities, compared with its equivalent in a synthetic grammar. For instance, Modern English *cottage* has only three formal possibilities: *cottage* (for subject or object function in the singular), *cottage's* (for possessive function in the singular or plural depending on the position of the apostrophe), *cottages* (for subject or object function in the plural).[1] In Latin the noun *casa* is a member of one of five separate declensions, each with its own formal conditions. The noun has seven formal possibilities: *casa* (subject function in the singular), *casae* (subject function in the plural, possessive and indirect object function in the singular), *casam* (direct object function in the singular), *casā* (instrumental function in the singular), *casārum* (possessive function in the plural), *casīs* (indirect object and instrumental function in the plural), and *casās* (direct object function in the plural). Nor do the formal complications end there. *Casa* is a member of the so-called "first" declension in Latin, wherein all the nouns show the same inflectional pattern, but where nearly all are grammatically "feminine"; that is, they are assigned gender which may or may not be natural to the concept in question. By our ordinary notions *cottage* is a neuter concept, the proof resting in our use of "it" as the appropriate pronoun here. So too with *silva* (forest), *porta* (gate), or *lingua* ((language), all feminines we would conceive as neuter. Modern English has all but done away with gram-

---

[1] Actually, the "sounded" formal possibilities for this noun are only two, since the sign of possession is an eye-sign only.

matical gender in favor of natural or logical gender. When we refer to a ship as "she," we are touching on grammatical gender, but it is not a vital dimension of Modern English as it is with synthetic languages.

Latin actually compromises between logical and grammatical gender, in that obviously male and female designations are treated as masculine or feminine. The noun *nauta* (sailor), though a first declension noun, is regarded as masculine, as is *agricola* (farmer). The Germanic languages, on the other hand, may push grammatical gender to what we regard as absurd positions. Modern German *Mädchen* (young woman or maiden) is construed as neuter. And Old English at times is no better in this respect: *wīfmann* (woman) is masculine, as are *stān* (stone) and *mōna* (moon).

The noun, then, in synthetic grammars, presents complitions unfamiliar to Modern English. The history of the noun in English language development is a history of simplification, in the three areas of case, number, and gender. To appreciate the nature of this simplification, we must examine some representative Old English nouns and their aspectual dimensions. Since Old English grammars, for better or worse, regularly use Latin terminology in discussing noun declension, it would be well at this point to clarify the following Latinisms.

Nominative refers to the subject function of a noun (or pronoun), and to the predicate noun (or adjective) function. Examples:

Wǣron *þā* ǣrest heora *lāttēowas* and *heretogan twēgen* gebrōþra, *Hengest* and *Horsa. Hī* wǣron Wihtgylses *suna*.

(Two brothers, Hengest and Horsa, were their first pilots and leaders. They were the sons of Wihtgyls.)

Bede's *History*

Swā bēop *þā fyrmestan ȳtemeste*, and *þā ȳtemestan fyrmeste*; sōþlīce *manige* sind *geclipode*, and *fēawe gecorene*. (Thus the first are last and the last first; truly, many are called and few chosen.)

Anglo-Saxon Gospels[2]

Genitive refers to the possessive function. In the examples above, the nouns *gebroþra* and *Wihtgylses* and the pronoun *heora* are possessives, as are the italicized in the following:

God wolde þā fandian *Abrahāmes* gehīersumnesse. (God then wished to test the obedience of Abraham.)

Ælfric

Ēalā, hū fela *hȳrlinga* on *mīnes fæder* hūse hlāf genōhne habbaþ . . . (Alas, how many workers in the house of my father have bread enough . . .)

Anglo-Saxon Gospels

Accusative refers to the direct object function and to the case of certain prepositional objects. In the examples above, the nouns *gehīersumnesse* and *hlāf* and the adjective *genōhne* are accusatives, as are the italicized in the following:

Nese: þȳlæs gē *þone hwǣte* āwyrtwalien, þonne gē *þone*

---

[2] The variety of inflectional endings for nominative, genitive, accusative, and dative cases will be accounted for in the discussion that follows of the various types or classes of declension.

coccel gadriaþ. (No, lest you uproot the wheat, when you gather the tares.)

Anglo-Saxon Gospels

Hēr Hengest and Æsc gefuhton wiþ *Wēalas,* and genāmon *unārīmedlicu hererēaf,* and þā Wēalas flugon þā *Engle* swā swā fȳr. (Here Hengest and Æsc fought against the Celts and took boundless booty, and the Celts fled from the English as if from fire.)

Anglo-Saxon Chronicle

Dative refers to the indirect object function, to the case of certain prepositional objects, and to the function of instrumentation or agency. In the examples above, the noun *hūse* is dative, as are the italicized in the following:

Hēr Hengest and Horsa fuhton wiþ *Wyrtgeorne þǣm cyninge* in þǣre stōwe þe is gecweden Ægles-þrep . . . (Here Hengest and Horsa fought against the king Vortigern in the place that is called Aylesford . . .)

Anglo-Saxon Chronicle

Gewordenre gecwidrǣdenne *þæm wyrhtum,* hē sealde *ælcum* ānne pening wiþ his dæges *weorce.* (An agreement having been made with the workers, he gave each one a penny for his day's work.)

Anglo-Saxon Gospels

And þæt folc þe hider cōm ongan weaxan and myclian tō *þan* swiþe þæt hī wǣron on *myclum ege þām sylfan landbīgengan* þe hī ǣr hider laþedon and cȳgdon. (And that folk that came hither began to grow and increase so strongly that they were a great terror to the inhabitants themselves who earlier invited and summoned them.)

Bede's *History*

As with Latin, Old English nouns are grouped in a number of declensions, according to the stem-ending of the noun in the primitive stage of the parent Germanic. It is possible to establish a broad division here between nouns with an original vocalic ending and those with a consonantal ending in the parent German, and convenient to label the vocalic group Class I and the consonantal group Class II. The following paradigms follow this classification.

Stān (stone) is a typical Class I masculine noun, which offers in its declension the basis for the regular remaining inflections of nearly all Modern English nouns:

	Singular		*Plural*
	stān	NOM.	stānas
	stānes	GEN.	stāna
	stāne	DAT.	stānum
	stān	ACC.	stānas

It may be noted here that the genitive singular and the nominative and accusative plural forms are identical with the Modern English equivalents in their consonant structure (*ST-N-S*). The vowels are different: the stem-vowel *A* has become *O*, and the *A* before the *S* of the plural has become *E* (changes that take place in early and late Middle English),[3] but the noun forms for the Old English are essentially familiar ones.

When we recognize that Old English is far more reliably

---

[3] The generally acknowledged chronology of English language history is Old English (450–1100), Middle English (1100–1500), Early Modern English (1500–1650). Like any consensus-chronology this one is arguable, but still quite useful for basic discussion.

spelled than Modern English, in that all spelled syllables
are sounded, even the forms of the nominative and accusative singular, which lack the unsounded -*e* of the modern
spelling, come home to us. The Old English dative singular,
with its spelled final -*e*, looks but does not sound familiar.
Only the genitive and dative plural forms here seem
essentially outside the pattern of the modern spelling and
sounding. The latter form, the dative, comes into line in
Middle English, as the result of a twofold process of levelling which may be observed taking place even in late Old
English (tenth and eleventh centuries). The short vowels
A-O-U lose their separate identity in a common short *E* (ə)
and the *M* nasal is no longer regularly distinguished from
the *N*, which in turn drops away as an inflection in Middle
English. Thus, *stānum* in late Old and early Middle English
might variously figure as *stānem*, *stānen*, *stānun*, before
becoming *stāne*, and then, by analogy with the nominative
and accusative plural forms, *stānes*.[4] So, too, with *stāna*,
stāne, *stānes*. By Chaucer's time, the various inflections of
stān have simplified to *stāne* and *stānes* and we have the
structure, if not the sound, of the modern noun.

The declension pattern of *stān* holds for a large number of
Old English nouns, among them *cyning* (king), *dæg* (day),
engel (angel), *dēofol* (devil), *fugol* (bird), *wealh* (foreigner),[5]
mearh (horse), *heofon* (heaven), *eorl* (nobleman), *gielp*

---

[4] For an excellent discussion of analogy as a linguistic phenomenon,
see G. L. Brook, *A History of the English Language*. Briefly, as Brook
puts it, "The result of the operation of linguistic analogy is to make
more complete the partial resemblance between two words."

[5] *Welsh* originally meant "alien" or "foreign" and was applied
by the Anglo-Saxons to the Celts in Britain.

(boasting), all of them grammatical masculines. There are in addition a group of masculines that very closely sub-scribe to the pattern, some (like *bæcere* [baker], *cyme* [arrival], *hyge* [mind], *mere* [lake], *mete* [food]) differing only in the -*e* ending of the nominative and accusative singular, others (mainly tribal names like *Dene* [Danes], *Engle* [English], *Myrce* [Mercians], *Seaxe* [Saxons]) in the -*e* ending of the nominative-accusative plural.

A second declension pattern for the Class I (vocalic) nouns in Old English is represented by the noun *scip* (ship), a grammatical neuter:

Singular		*Plural*
scip	NOM.	scipu
scipes	GEN.	scipa
scipe	DAT.	scipum
scip	ACC.	scipu

The noun resembles *stān* in all respects save the nominative and accusative plural. The -*u* inflection here would level to -*e*, and the modern -*s* inflection for the plural forms would again come about through analogy. (It might here be noted that about 45 percent of all nouns in Classes I and II in Old English are grammatical masculines; and the great majority of these masculines are in Class I. Thus, the frequency of the -*es* and -*as* inflections for the Old English noun is considerable and underscores the analogy operation.)

The third declension pattern for Class I nouns involves grammatical feminines and may be illustrated by *glōf* (glove):

Singular		Plural
glōf	NOM.	glōfa
glōfe	GEN.	glōfa
glōfe	DAT.	glōfum
glōfe	ACC.	glōfa

Here the pattern of inflection is at once simpler than that for *stān* and less familiar. When one appreciates that many feminines resembling *glōf* show -*e* instead of -*a* for the nominative and accusative plural forms, it is obvious that the feminine group of Class I nouns represents the lightest inflectional pattern in the earliest stage of English, limited to -*e*/-*a* and -*um*.

The nouns in Class II, which showed a consonantal ending in the parent Germanic, belong to all three grammatical genders. The following three illustrate masculine, neuter, and feminine, respectively:

Nama (name)

Singular		Plural
nama	NOM.	naman
naman	GEN.	namana
naman	DAT.	namum
naman	ACC.	naman

Ēare (ear)

ēare	NOM.	ēaran
ēaran	GEN.	ēarena
ēaran	DAT.	ēarum
ēare	ACC.	ēaran

Eorþe (earth)

eorþe	NOM.	eorþan
eorþan	GEN.	eorþena
eorþan	DAT.	eorþum
eorþan	ACC.	eorþan

An is clearly the dominant inflection here, figuring in all four cases (nominative plural, genitive singular, dative singular, and accusative singular and plural). Considering that a substantial number of Old English nouns belonged to Class II, it is noteworthy that plurals like *oxen* are the only Modern English nouns that show the direct survival of this inflection. It is also noteworthy that Modern English *children* and *brethen* represent a fusion of two kinds of plural inflection: the *-en* taken over from Class II and appended to the *-ru* that was their original (irregular) plural inflection.

In addition to these two main classes, there are certain irregular declensions in Old English, the most interesting from the modern point of view being the so-called mutation declension. The masculine *fōt* (foot) and the feminine *gōs* (goose) will illustrate this:

Singular		*Plural*
fōt	NOM.	fēt
fōtes	GEN.	fōta
fēt	DAT.	fōtum
fōt	ACC.	fēt
gōs	NOM.	gēs
gōse	GEN.	gōsa
gēs	DAT.	gōsum
gōs	ACC.	gēs

These are clearly the antecedents of the modern *foot/feet*, *goose/geese*, but with a peculiar difference. The stem-vowel does not remain constant for singular or plural; that of the dative singular resembles the nominative and accusative plural, and that of the remaining singular forms resembles the genitive and dative plural. This holds true for the nouns within the Old English group, some of which—*bōc* (book), *frēond* (friend), *āc* (oak), *burg* (fortress)—have since passed over to the *stān* pattern.

The masculine declension pattern for Class I, illustrated by *stān*, is clearly the basis for what regular noun inflection still exists in English. If we look to the state of the noun in Middle English, taking the East Midland dialect derived from the Old English Mercian and the basis of Modern Standard English, we note that by Chaucer's time (fourteenth century) the noun is pretty well established in its modern sense. For the great majority of Chaucerian nouns -*s* or -*es* is the regular genitive singular and common plural inflection. Some few nouns retain the Old English dative singular -*e* (*on lyve*, *on fyre*, *with childe*), but the regular Old English dative plural -*um* has levelled successively as -*em*, -*en*, -*e* and finally lost its identity in the common plural -*s*/-*es*. In earlier Middle English (twelfth and thirteenth centuries), especially in the Southern dialect derived from the Old English West Saxon, there are numerous plurals in -*en*, survivors of the Old English Class II declension, e.g., *voan* (foes), *honden* (hands), *deoflen* (devils), *goddeden* (good deeds), *hennen* (hens), *sunnen* (sins), *freren* (friars), all of which later pass over to the Class I plural pattern.

CHAPTER FIVE

Pronoun History

Pronoun forms are traditionally grouped as personal, possessive, reflexive, demonstrative, interrogative, and indefinite; and perhaps it is well to maintain these classifications for purposes of discussion of English pronoun history. One must note, however, that pronoun development in early English is far from uniform for these various categories. For some, such as the personal pronoun, the inflections have been quite well preserved. For others, such as the demonstratives, erosion has been considerable. Let us consider the groups in turn, using the Old English paradigms as a basis.

The personal pronoun in Old English includes the noun concepts of number, case, and gender, and additionally that of person: *first* (I/we), *second* (you), and *third* (he/she/it/they). Number involves an aspect familiar to students of certain modern European languages but long gone from English, the *dual*, a set of forms used to indicate a special two-person relationship. The French second person form *tu* or the German *du* convey something like the sense of the Old English. (Obviously, a proper young Frenchwoman would balk, officially at least, at being addressed as *tu* on a first date.) In Old English, a full set of dual forms exist but are seldom encountered even at this early stage. In Ælfric's *Genesis*, Abraham addresses or refers to Isaac in the dual, but we may fairly assume that this special numerical concept was on its way out of the language even in its beginnings.[1] The Old English personal pronoun is declined as follows:

FIRST PERSON

	Singular	*Dual*	*Plural*
NOM.	ic	wit	wē
GEN.	mīn	uncer	ūre
DAT.	mē	unc	ūs
ACC.	mē	unc	ūs

SECOND PERSON

	Singular	*Dual*	*Plural*
NOM.	þū	git	gē
GEN.	þīn	incer	ēower
DAT.	þē	inc	ēow
ACC.	þē	inc	ēow

---

[1] We may assume, however, that the dual played some regular or considerable part in the parent Germanic.

THIRD PERSON

	Singular			Common Plural
	masc.	fem.	neuter	
NOM.	hē	hēo	hit	hīe
GEN.	his	hire	his	hiera
DAT.	him	hire	him	him
ACC.	hine	hīe	hit	hīe

A glance at these forms will reveal numerous obvious transferences into our modern speech. The first person forms *mine, me, we, our, us*; the second person *you, your*;[2] the third person *he, his, him, her* are all fairly apparent from the Old English. We must account then for the seemingly exceptional or unusual forms here.

Ic will not seem strange to the student of modern German; it is pronounced very like *ich*. Interestingly, the conservative Germanic Icelandic has a velar *k* in its first person masculine nominative, e.g., *ek*, certainly the proto-Germanic velar for the form, and the Germanic equivalent to Indo-European velar G (ego) under Grimm's Law. Modern English *I*, then, represents the end of a process of elimination: *ik, ic, I,* with Icelandic and modern German retaining the hard and soft consonants accompanying the vowel.

Analogy must account for the displacement of *gē* by *ēow* in the second person plural nominative, and likewise *hine* by *him* in the third person masculine accusative. The modern feminine *she* has never been fully accounted for, but it may

[2] Other of these forms, e.g., *þū, þīn, þē, gē,* survive today as Quakerisms.

reasonably be considered a fusion of the Old English third person feminine nominative *hēo* and *sēo*, a feminine nominative from the demonstrative pronoun declension.[3] The neuter *hit* was to lose its initial *h* in Middle English, although Chaucer and early Modern English occasionally disclose the older form, which still survives in the rustic American South ("Hit looks like rain"). The modern neuter possessive *its* may be accounted for by analogy with -*'s* from the Old English Class I noun declension (*it's* was the usual spelling for the form until about 1800); and it must have had to do with the decline in early English of grammatical gender and the desire to distinguish the natural neuter from the masculine. We find *it* ("by it young") and *his* ("that little candle throws his beams") as neuter possessives in Shakespeare.

The third person plural forms always occasion comment in that the Modern English *they, their, them* are Scandinavian (*þei, þeir, þeim*) replacements of the Old English. If the Old English forms had prevailed we would today employ *hi, here, hem*. Late Middle English sometimes offers a combination of the two languages: *thei, here, hem*.

The Old English possessive pronouns are mainly the genitive forms of the personal pronouns, e.g., *mīn, þīn, ūre, ēower, his*. An old reflexive form *sīn* sometimes functions for the third person possessive concept, masculine and feminine singular and plural. The possessive adjective forms (*my, thy*) develop in Middle English as the result of the pronominal -*n* dropping out, first when followed by nouns beginning with a consonant, then eventually by any nouns.

[3] We assume here the need to distinguish the feminine *hēo* from *hē*.

Early Modern English occasionally shows the pronoun ending in the adjective position (*mine* host), but since the seventeenth century the pronoun and adjective forms for the possessive have been regularly distinguished.

The history of the reflexive is a fusion of *self*, originally an adjective, with a preceding pronoun. Old English *ic self* is nominative for both pronoun and adjective. The modern equivalent *myself* suggests that somewhere in its development (probably in late Middle English) *self* was regarded as a noun modified by the possessive adjective. So too with *ourselves, yourself*, and *yourselves*. Thus, the occasionally heard, and grammatically "incorrect" *hisself* would appear to be logical for the third person; the regularly accepted *himself* actually casts *self* back into its original adjective role.[4]

The demonstrative pronoun in Old English consists of two sets of forms. These forms do a kind of double duty as adjectives or articles. The paradigms are as follows:

se (that, the)

	Singular			*Common Plural*
	masc.	*fem.*	*neuter*	
NOM.	se	sēo	þæt	þā
GEN.	þæs	þære	þæs	þāra
DAT.	þǣm	þære	þǣm	þǣm
ACC.	þone	þā	þæt	þā

[4] In the Biblical "Ætīewede se coccel *hine*" (the cockle showed itself, lit. *him*), we get the original sense of the pronominal reflexive.

þes (this)

	Singular			*Common Plural*
	masc.	fem.	neuter	
NOM.	þes	þēos	þis	þās
GEN.	þisses	þisse	þisses	þissa
DAT.	þissum	þisse	þissum	þissum
ACC.	þisne	þās	þis	þās

When we recognize that *se* and *þes* survive in Modern English only through the neuter singular nominative and accusative, we are confronted with perhaps the most extreme simplification in inflection in all of English language history. The modern German still has its *der, die, das* complication for the definite article, and the Romance languages have their gender agreement between definite article and noun; but Modern English takes the article for granted as probably the simplest of all grammatical concepts. In Old English the *se* declension, especially, is wide ranging indeed. Its forms could particularize, in the modern demonstrative sense ("*þæt* was god cyning," that was a good king), or simply function as a personal pronoun. The following sentence from the *St. Matthew Gospel* illustrates usage of *se* as both a personal and relative pronoun and as an article, and also shows *þes* as an adjective: "Ǣlc þāra þe þās mīn word gehīerþ, and þā wyrcþ, biþ gelīc þ̄ǣm wīsan were, sē his hūs ofer stān getimbrode." (Each of those that hear these my words and follow [lit., work] them, be like the wise man who built his house on stone.) *þāra* (of those), a genitive plural, is a personal pronoun here, possessing Ǣlc (each). *þā* (them) is also a personal pronoun, with *word* (words) as its accusative neuter plural antecedent.

þǣm (the) is a definite article, modifying the dative masculine singular *were* (man).[5] *Se* (who) is a relative pronoun,
having reference to *were* in the main clause. *þās* (these), as a
form of *þes*, functions as an adjective here, modifying *word*.
The place of *se* in early English grammar is further complicated by the fact that while it yields the Modern English
that from the neuter singular, we must look elsewhere for our
modern *the*. The most frequently used relative pronoun in
Old English is the undeclined *þe* (who/which/that). By
analogy with this form, and from the initial *þ* of many of
its singular and plural forms, *se* becomes *þe* in Middle
English.[6]

In addition to the above paradigms for *se* and *þes*, there
exist for each in the singular, separate instrumental forms.
þȳ and *þȳs* are among the few distinct instrumental forms
in Old English, where the dative case regularly includes the
instrumental function. Thus, in the Modern English *the
sooner the better*, the first article goes back to the notion of
þȳ sōnra: (because) the sooner (therefore) the better.

The Modern English interrogative pronouns *who*, *which*,
and *what* derive from Old English *hwā*, *hwylc*, and *hwæt*. The
paradigms for the first and third of these are clearly related,
as masculine and neuter respectively:

	masc.		*neut.*
	hwā	NOM.	hwæt
	hwæs	GEN.	hwæs
	hwǣm	DAT.	hwǣm
	hwone	ACC.	hwæt

[5] Cp. the early Modern English "like unto the man."

[6] A phrase like *ye olde hocke shoppe* actually shows a misreading of
þe and has nothing to do with any historical *y* sound here.

Hwylc is patterned according to one of the two Old English adjective declensions.[7] Our modern adverbs *why* and *how* were originally instrumental forms in the interrogative declensions. *Who* deserves comment in that, unlike *what*, it broadens its function from interrogative to relative.[8] For Middle English, the neuter singular *þæt*, from the *se* declension, served as the basis for a general relative for all genders, much as *þe* had for Old English. In early Modern English *who* and *whom* (from the dative singular of *hwā*) occur as relatives ("Who steals my purse steals trash," "her Maiestie, whom abruptely he termeth Elysa"). *Which*, too, assumed a relative function in early Modern English, mainly for neuter antecedents (but note "Our Father, *which* art in heaven").

The indefinite pronoun forms in Old English are quite numerous and may best be represented as evidence of a particular strength of the earliest phase of the language, the development of compounds. Around the roots *hwā*, *hwæþer* (lit., whether, which of two), *hwylc*, and *wiht* (whit/wight) are built the following: *æghwā* (each one), *æthwā* (each one), *ahwā* (any one), *gehwā* (every one); *æghwæþer* (each of two), *ahwæþer/ohwæþer/awþer/owþer* (either one), *hahwæþer/nohwæþer/nawþer/nowþer* (neither one); *æghwelc* (each one), *gehwilc* (every one), *hwelchwugu* (some one), *samhwilc* (some); *awiht/owiht/awuht/owuht/aht/oht* (lit., aught, anything), *nawiht/nowiht/nawuht/nowuht/naht/noht* (lit.,

<hr/>

[7] For the distinction between strong and weak adjective forms in Old English, cf. chapter seven.

[8] Shakespeare's "*What* you will" suggests the indefinite dimension to that pronoun.

nought, nothing). The variant spellings here illustrate the simplification of compounding. Other indefinites that yield modern pronoun forms are *ǣlc* (each), *ǣnig/nǣnig* (any/not any), *ān/nān* (one/none).

CHAPTER SIX

Verb History

Unlike the early English noun, which poses formal problems relatively unfamiliar to the student of Modern English, the early English verb may be studied in a generally familiar context, that of "regular" and "irregular," or "weak" and "strong." Every modern schoolboy knows that the overwhelming majority of Modern English verbs develop their tense patterns through the addition of *-ed* to the unchanged stem, and that a few verbs (heavy duty performers, for the most part) show tense changes through a change in the verb stem itself: *ride, rode, ridden.* What the schoolboy probably does not know is that this twofold patterning of modern verbs has its roots in the Germanic background of English, and that Old English, as a Germanic dialect, manifests precisely these same conditions, altered in proportion perhaps but essentially like.

It should be noted at the outset that each verb pattern has three convenient and related defining terms. *Regular* verbs are so called because they make up something over 99 percent of the total Modern English verb-stock. They are called *weak* rather fancifully, because they indicate tense change externally, lacking, one might speculate, the intestinal fortitude to change internally. (The verb-stem in *walk, walked, walked*, after all, does not act; it is acted upon from without.) The third defining term for this class of verbs, *suffix*, refers to the dental *-ed* (regularly pronounced *t*), which is the standard addition to the verb-stem. The *irregular* verbs (irregular because there are only about one hundred and sixty such verbs among the thousands in Modern English) are *strong* because they change internally, without outside help. They are also called *ablaut* verbs in recognition of their Germanic nature (the Germanic term means vowel-gradation or the change in the radical vowel in a series of related root syllables). The vowel gradation in *ride, rode, ridden* is an ī/o/i ablaut, or internal sound change.

I

Perhaps it is well to begin with the strong verbs. About half of the total number of 330 in Old English survive today. Some of the original stock crossed over to the weak group (*burn*—originally *byrnan, barn, burnon, burnen*—and *help*—originally *helpan, healp, hulpon, holpen*—are examples) and others have disappeared from English (*snīþan*, to cut, and *niman*, to take, survive in modern German cognates, *schneiden* and *nehmen*). In one important aspect, the Old

English strong verbs differ from their modern descendants: where there are regularly three "principal parts" (infinitive, past, past participle) to a Modern English verb (strong or weak), there are four to the earlier verb. Thus, *ride, rode, ridden* would be *rīdan, rād, ridon, riden* in Old English. *Rād* and *ridon* are the past tense[1] roots for singular and plural. We should note here the essential and regular features of the principal parts of the Old English verb. The *-an* attached to the stem *rīd-* is the indication of the infinitive (cp. German *-en*, or Latin *-āre, -ēre, -ere, -īre*), and it applies to strong or weak verbs. The *-on* inflection is the regular sign of the past-plural condition for strong and weak verbs. The *-en* inflection defines the strong past-participial form.

A conjugation of *rīdan* will further clarify verb structure, as to tense (present and past),[2] number (singular and plural), and person (first, second, and third):

PRESENT INDICATIVE

	Singular		Plural
First Person	ic	rīde	wē rīdaþ
Second Person	þū	rīd(e)st	gē rīdaþ
Third Person	hē, hēo, hit	rīd(e)þ	hīe rīdaþ

PAST INDICATIVE

	Singular		Plural
First Person	ic	rād	wē ridon
Second Person	þū	ride	gē ridon
Third Person	hē	rād	hīe ridon

[1] *Preterit* is a common alternate term for the past tense concept, especially for Germanic grammar.

[2] Old English lacks distinctive future-tense forms; the present forms may be interpreted as future in appropriate contexts.

PRESENT SUBJUNCTIVE

	Singular	Plural
First Person	ic rīde	wē rīden
Second Person	þū rīde	gē rīden
Third Person	hē rīde	hīe rīden

PAST SUBJUNCTIVE

	Singular	Plural
First Person	ic ride	wē riden
Second Person	þū ride	gē riden
Third Person	hē ride	hīe riden

PRESENT PARTICIPLE	PAST PARTICIPLE
rīdend	riden

The present indicative inflections survive past Middle English into early Modern English, e.g., *ridest*, *rideth*, though *rideth* loses something of its original plural emphasis. The past indicative shows the second person singular sharing the stem of the past plural forms; the first and third person singular stem, however, is ultimately to survive as the single stem for all past tense forms, singular and plural. The subjunctive forms, it will be noted, are relatively simpler than the indicatives, with -*e* and -*en* serving as the inflections for both tenses: an interesting anticipation of the Modern English subjunctive, which in theory is fairly complicated but formally much less so. The original present participial form of the verb, with its -*end* inflection, is alien to our sense of the form. We derive our -*ing* from the early Germanic -*ung*, a substantive inflectional concept that survives in *Achtung* (Action), *Hoffnung* (Hope).

Rīdan is only one of a series of related strong verbs in Old English. It is regularly described as a Class I strong verb: all verbs in this group share the ī/ā/i ablaut row.[3] Other examples are as follows:

Infinitive	Past Singular	Past Plural	Past Participle
risan (rise)	ras	rison	risen
drīfan (drive)	drāf	drifon	drifen
bīdan (bide)	bād	bidon	biden
glīdan (glide)	glād	glidon	gliden

There are six other groupings of Old English strong verbs, which may be summarized as follows:

Class II verbs share an ablaut row of ēo/ēa/u/o:[4]

bēodan (bid)	bēad	budon	boden
clēofan (cleave)	clēaf	clufon	clofen
smēocan (smoke)	smēac	smucon	smocen
rēocan (reek)	rēac	rucon	rocen

Verbs in Class III are grouped according to the consonant structure of the stem. Regularly, Class III verbs share a nasal or a liquid plus a second (non-nasal, non-liquid) consonant in the stem:[5]

---

[3] Except for certain "contract" forms (e.g., *þēon*, prosper), where one must assume the earlier presence of the vowel row.

[4] Here, too, certain forms (e.g., *flēon*, flee) represent a contraction of an earlier form.

[5] Here, the vowel row may differ, depending on whether the first consonant is liquid or nasal.

	Past	*Past*	*Past*
Infinitive	*Singular*	*Plural*	*Participle*
bin*d*an (bind)	band	bundon	bunden
he*lp*an (help)	healp	hulpon	holpen
weo*rp*an (throw)	wearp	wurpon	worpen
weo*rþ*an (become)	wearþ	wurdon	worden
gy*lp*an (boast)	gealp	gulpon	golpen

Class IV and Class V verbs generally resemble those of Class III in that the consonant structure of the stem determines the grouping. Class IV types show a single stem-consonant, either a nasal or a liquid:

cu*m*an (come)	cōm	cōmon	cumen
ni*m*an (take)	nōm	nōmon	numen
be*r*an (bear)	bær	bǣron	boren

Verbs in Class V also show a single stem-consonant other than a nasal or liquid:

me*t*an (measure)	mæt	mǣton	meten
tre*d*an (tread)	træd	trǣdon	treden
spre*c*an (speak)	spræc	sprǣcon	sprecen
gi*f*an (give)	geaf	gēafon	gifen

Class VI verbs are classified by the ablaut row a/ō/ō/a:[6]

fa*r*an (journey)	fōr	fōron	faren
slean (strike)	slōg	slōgon	slagen[7]
wa*d*an (go)	wōd	wōdon	waden

[6] Only the verbs of Classes VI and VII disclose an identical stem-vowel for their preterit singular and plural forms.

[7] The preterit and past-participial forms here suggest that *slay* and *slug* are ancient relatives.

Class VII verbs show no simple or evident rationale for classification, but rather an original similarity in the common Germanic preterit forms. This condition is called reduplication because the initial stem consonant is repeated medially, as in *heht*, an early preterit of *hātan* (call) and *reord*, a preterit of *rǣdan* (advise). (The second *h* in *heht* discloses this condition.) But the standard Old English forms have contracted and the reduplication is only evident in the lengthened stem vowel.

hātan (call)	hēt	hēton	haten
lǣtan (let)	lēt	lēton	lǣten
bēatan (beat)	bēot	bēoton	bēaten

At this point it is relevant to emphasize once more the commonality of the Germanic language group through the obvious cognate relationships among the strong verbs. The following chart for the first six classes of strong verbs in Old English, Gothic, and Old Norse will testify to this point:

OLD ENGLISH, GOTHIC, AND OLD NORSE STRONG VERBS

Class

I	OE	bīdan (bide)	bād	bidon	biden
	G	beidan	baiþ	bidun	bidans
	ON	bīþa	beiþ	biþu	beþinn
II	OE	bēodan (bid)	bēad	budon	boden
	G	biudan	bauþ	budun	budans
	ON	bjoþa	bauþ	buþu	boþinn

OLD ENGLISH, GOTHIC, AND OLD NORSE STRONG VERBS

Class

III	OE	bindan (bind)	band	bundon	bunden
	G	bindan	band	bundun	bundans
	ON	binda	batt	bundu	bundinn
	OE	helpan (help)	healp	hulpon	holpen
	G	hilpan	halp	hulpun	hulpans
	ON	helpa	halp	hulpu	holpinn
IV	OE	beran (bear)	bær	bǣron	boren
	G	bairan	bar	bērun	baurans
	ON	bera	bar	bāru	borinn
V	OE	metan (measure)	mæt	mǣton	meten
	G	mitan	mat	mētun	mitans
	ON	meta	māt	mātu	metinn
VI	OE	faran (travel)	fōr	fōron	faren
	G	faran	fōr	fōrun	forans
	ON	fara	fōr	foru	farinn

II

The Old English weak verbs, though far more numerous, are much easier to classify. Essentially there are two closely related types, differing only in the vowel of the suffix. The Class I weak verbs may be illustrated in the principal parts of *fremman* (do, perform): *fremman, fremede, gefremed*. It will be noted here that the infinitive inflection is the simple -*an*, and the inflections for the preterit and past participle the dental -*ed* (e). Class II weak verbs resemble Class I, except that the vowel in the infinitive inflection is a diphthong and the vowel of the past tense forms is *o* rather than *e*; e.g., *endian* (end), *endode, geendod*. A third group of weak verbs consists of four important concepts: *habban* (have), *libban* (live), *secgan* (say), and *hycgan* (think). These actually show some variation in the stem vowel for the various tenses (e.g., *habban, hæfde, gehæfd; hycgan, hogde, gehogod*) but at least some of the forms in the present tense of these verbs share the stem-vowel of the past tense forms (first person singular *hæbbe*, second person singular *hogast*).

The conjugation of *fremman* will serve as a model for typical weak verbs:

PRESENT INDICATIVE

	Singular	*Plural*
First Person	ic fremme	wē fremmaþ
Second Person	þū fremest	gē fremmaþ
Third Person	hē, hēo, hit fremeþ	hīe fremmaþ

PAST INDICATIVE

	Singular	*Plural*
First Person	ic fremede	wē fremedon
Second Person	þū fremedest	gē fremedon
Third Person	hē fremede	hīe fremedon

PRESENT SUBJUNCTIVE

	Singular	*Plural*
First Person	ic fremme	wē fremmen
Second Person	þū fremme	gē fremmen
Third Person	hē fremme	hīe fremmen

PAST SUBJUNCTIVE

	Singular	*Plural*
First Person	ic fremede	wē fremeden
Second Person	þū fremede	gē fremeden
Third Person	hē fremede	hīe fremeden

PRESENT PARTICIPLE	PAST PARTICIPLE
fremmende	gefremed

In addition to the strong and weak classification, there are a number of Old English verbs that must be considered anomalous. *Bēon/wesan* (to be) is one, involving as it does four separate stems: *bēo, bist, biþ, bēoþ* (present singular and plural); *ēom, eart, is* (present singular) and *sindon* (present plural); *sīe, sīen* (subjunctive forms); and *wæs, wēre, wēron* (past singular and plural). *Gan* (go) is a second such verb, with its preterit forms built on the separate root *eod-* (surviving in Chaucerian times as *yede*), a root later to be displaced by the equally anomalous *went* (from Old English *wendan*, to turn). Another irregular grouping comprises the preterit-present verbs, so called because the present-tense forms derive from original strong preterits and weak preterits develop to fill the gap. *Witan* (to know) is an example: the present tense (ic/hē) *wat* and (þū) *wast* are in form first class strong preterits, and the past tense (ic/hē) *wiste*, (þū) *wistest*, (wē/gē/hīe) *wiston* with the dental *t* pattern like weak preterit forms.

III

By Chaucer's time, the English verb had in certain important respects settled into a pattern quite recognizable

to the modern student. The Old English plural inflection *-on*
had become *-en*, with the *n* dispensable. The singular
inflections *-est* and *-eth* remain, as they do into Elizabethan
English. Thus, the fourteenth century conjugation of *ride*
would involve only four inflections (*e, est, eth, en*) compared
with seven in the Old English (*e, est, e, a, on, en, an*).
Perhaps the most interesting single feature of the fourteenth
century verb is the flexible state of the infinitive formation.
The Old English infinitive indicator *-an* survives as *-en*, but
the auxiliary *to* finds frequent employment. Thus, in the
first hundred-odd lines of Chaucer's *Canterbury Tales*
Prologue we find the following infinitive constructions, all
of which would necessitate the inflection *-an* in Old English
syntax:

> Thanne longen folk *to goon* on pilgrimages,
> And palmeres for *to seken* straunge strondes
> (as infinitives governed by *longen, goon* and *seken* show
> both the old infinitive inflection and the new auxiliary *to*)

> They wende,
> The hooly blisful martir for *to seke*
> (uninflected infinitive *to seke* governed by *wende*)

> That toward Caunterbury wolden *ryde*
> (as governed by *wolden*, the infinitive *ryde* shows neither
> auxiliary nor inflection)

> And made forward early for *to ryse*
> (auxiliary, no inflection)

> fro the tyme that he first began
> *To riden* out
> (both auxiliary and inflection)

for *to tellen* yow of his array
(auxiliary and inflection)

He koude songes *make* and wel *endite*
(neither auxiliary nor inflection for infinitives governed
by *koude*)

for him liste *ride* so
(neither auxiliary nor inflection for infinitive governed by
liste)

Wel koude he *dresse*
(neither auxiliary nor inflection for infinitive governed
by *koude*)

Clearly, the language at this point has neither definitely
discarded the inflection nor settled on *to*.

With the sixteenth century, verb usage is virtually
stabilized in familiar modern terms, but there are certain
exceptional areas. One is the third person singular, regularly
-eth in Chaucer. The inflection persists in Elizabethan
English but *s* is increasingly used and becomes standard in
the early seventeenth century. Thus, Shakespeare's Portia
says of mercy, "It *blesseth* him that *gives* and him that
takes." In Shakespeare, too, we find a rather free structuring
of participial forms, with the regular *-en* inflection for
strong verbs discarded: "Have you *chose* this man" (*Corio-
lanus*); "And thereupon these errors are *arose*" (*Comedy of
Errors*); "Then, Brutus, I have much *mistook* your passion"
(*Julius Caesar*); "Thou hast *eat* thy bearer up" (*2 Henry
IV*); "*Writ* in remembrance more than things long past"
(*Richard II*). Strong and weak verb distinctions are sometimes tentative for the period; *waxed* and *waxen*, *sowed* and

sew, *helped* and *holp*, along with weak forms like *growed*, *shrinked*, and *swinged* testify to this. Finally, in the plays and poems of Shakespeare we note the formation of verbs from nouns and adjectives: "Which *happies* those that pay the willing loan" (*Sonnet VI*); "Such stuff as madmen *tongue* and *brain* not" (*Cymbeline*); "Which pitifully *disaster* the cheeks" (*Antony and Cleopatra*); "This day shall *gentle* his condition" (*Henry V*); "*Lesson* me" (*Two Gentlemen of Verona*). In the era of the Inkhorn controversy, the conservative-radical quarrel over vocabulary, it is fitting that its greatest writer should thus experiment in verb-thinking.

CHAPTER SEVEN

Early English Syntax

The foregoing chapters on the noun, pronoun, and verb have at least implied problems of syntax, of phrase, clause, or sentence structure in the history of early English. In this final chapter, we will consider some of these, following through as it were with the terms and conditions of synthetic-analytic grammar set forth in chapter two. There we noted in two Old English passages, one poetry (*Beowulf*) and the other prose (*St. Matthew*), that while the earliest stage of our language is not utterly alien to our modern word-ordering, there is a significantly different emphasis. The meaning of the Old English sentence is derived from a recognition of inflectional relationships rather than a "set" word order, reversal of which may cause reversal of meaning. This synthesis of inflectional relationships is the very essence of a grammar like Old English; the realization that a noun or pronoun form is an accusative rather than a dative or a genitive may, in a modern translation, keep an early hero from braining himself rather than someone else.

Our survey of early syntax will be selective here, concentrating on those syntactic aspects that most pertain to the primary parts of speech—noun, pronoun, verb—already treated. For noun and pronoun, *modification* and *agreement* will be considered, and for the verb *mood* and *voice*.

I

The student of any of the Romance languages soon becomes aware of an aspect of noun/pronoun and modifier agreement absent in Modern English, the difference in the adjective form depending on the number and gender of the noun/pronoun modified. The French "Le garçon est *petit*" and "La fille est *petite*," "Les garçons sont *petits*," "Les filles sont *petites*" simply illustrate the point. This kind of agreement is even more emphatic in the Germanic languages, where an adjective not only agrees with its governing noun/pronoun in number and gender but also is declined differently, depending on its syntactic position. In Old English, the adjective is declined like a Class II type of noun (cf. chapter four) if it follows a demonstrative or a possessive, e.g., "under þām *cealdan* waeter" (under the cold water), "on þǣre *ilcan* nihte" (on the same night), "þurh þæs *ilcan* cyninges bebod" (through the same king's bidding). It is declined much like a Class I type of noun if no such modification precedes it, or if it is positioned as a predicate adjective, e.g., "uppan *ānre* dūne" (upon a hill), "mid *heofonlicre* blētsunge" (with heavenly blessing), "his hryre wæs *micel*" (his fall was great), "Swā bēoþ þā fyrmestan *ȳtemeste*" (So be the first last). Chaucerian English preserves this syntactic distinction for adjectives, though the forms themselves are much simplified: we find the spelling *yonge* when that adjective follows an article, demonstrative or possessive, but *yong* when the adjective is predicative.

Agreement between adjectives and nouns/pronouns may perhaps best be noted in constructions employing the past participle as modifier. Here, depending on the number of the noun/pronoun, the participle itself may be inflected, e.g., "manige sind *geclipode*, and fēawe *gecorene*" (many are called but few chosen). *Geclipode* and *gecorene* are weak and strong past-participial forms, respectively; and the final *e* is due to the plurals *manige* and *fēawe*. (Cp. "sē wæs on Rōme *gelǣred*" [who was taught in Rome], "ānne ramm betwix þǣm brēmlum be þǣm hornum *gehǣft*" [a ram caught by the horns between the brambles].) By the fourteenth century, this distinction is lost, as in the Wycliffite "many be *clepid*, but fewe ben *chosun*."

Another area of agreement relates to nouns/pronouns and verbs. In Old English, a compound subject may take a singular verb form, if the members of the compound are singular. And such a subject may in part precede and in part follow the verb, e.g., "þā *cōm* þǣr *regen* and micel *flōd*" (then rain and great flooding came there), "And æfter þǣm *Hengest fēng* to rīce, and *Æsc* his sunu" (And after this Hengest and Æsc his son came to rule), "þær *sceal* beon *gedrync* and *plega*" (there shall be drinking and sport). And very occasionally the opposite may occur, as in *Beowulf*,

11.905 and 2164, where plural subjects (*sorhwylmas*, grief-surgings; *mearas*, horses) agree with singular verbs (*lemede*, oppressed; *weardode*, occupied). In Middle English, another kind of anomaly in subject-verb agreement anticipates an occasional Elizabethan construction. In the writings of the Yorkshire mystic Richard Rolle (early fourteenth century), we encounter "Til men or wymen þat *takes* þam til actife lyfe, twa thynges *falles*." *Takes* and *falles* must be construed as plural verb forms. So too in Shakespeare: "troubled minds that *wakes*" (*Rape of Lucrece*), "Whose own hard dealings teaches them" (*Merchant of Venice*).

II

As noted in chapter six, the Old English verb has distinct forms for only the present and past tenses, not the future. The latter is inferred from present-tense forms in future context, e.g., "Ic *arīse* and ic *fare* tō mīnum fæder, and ic *secge* him: 'Ēalā, fæder, ic syngode.' " (I [will] arise and [will] go to my father and I [will] say to him: "Alas, father, I have sinned.")

The Old English *sculan* (have to, be obliged to) and *willan* (wish to) by the twelfth century have assumed their familiar future tense function, as in the *Ancren Riwle*: "*Ichchulle* vor þe luve of þe *nimen* þis fiht upon me" (I shall for love of you take this fight upon myself), "ich *schal* betweonen ham *undervongen* deaþes wunde" (I shall between them receive a mortal wound).

If futurity is only implied in Old English, rather than indicated through specific forms, the past-tense system of this earliest stage of the language is nothing like as complicated as it eventually becomes. The particular preterit forms of Old English serve for past perfect concepts (often introduced by _ǣr_, before); and while _have_ and _had_ do figure in Old English as auxiliaries in verb phrases involving transitive verbs, it is only with Middle English that _have_ figures in the perfect tenses of intransitive verbs as well. The progressive tense forms built on the suffix _-ing_ only become current in the sixteenth century, and then after a long and complicated development from an original substantive status (e.g., Old English _fēding_, feeding).

Mood as an aspect of the Old English verb was rather more complicated, though never comparable to Latin and Greek, where the subjunctive is certainly one of the greatest single formal complications in the study of those languages. Basically, the Old English subjunctive indicates subjective conditions, of which three in particular may be noted here: (a) clauses expressing desire or command; (b) clauses dependent on verbs of saying or thinking; (c) clauses indicating supposition. The first of these, on the model of Marie Antoinette's "Let them eat cake," may quite naturally figure in royal decree (in which desire and command are as one): "_Forhtien_ and _ondrǣden_ ealle eorþ-būende Daniēles God" (Let all earth-dwellers fear and dread Daniel's God); or prayer: "_sīe_ þīn nama gehālgod" (be thy name hallowed).

The second, often termed indirect question or discourse, is very common, involving as it does the rephrasing of a (hypothetical) direct quotation: "And þā þe þǣr ǣrest cōmon wēndon þæt hie _scolden_ māre onfōn" (And they that first came there supposed that they should receive more); "hēo hine . . . lǣrde, þæt hē weoroldhād _forlēte_ and

monuchāde *onfēnge*" (she taught him that he should aban-
don the secular condition and embrace the monastic).

The third, on the model of "If I were king," is doubtless
the most familiar to the modern student, since this is
virtually the only subjective condition we continue to label
as such: "Nese: þȳlǣs gē þone hwǣte *āwyrtwaliēn*, þonne gē
þone coccel gadriaþ" (Not so: lest you should uproot the
wheat, when you gather the tares); "swylce eal Finnsburh
fȳrenu *wǣre*" (as if all Finnsburg were on fire). The Old
English subjunctive inflections, limited as they are to *e* and
en, may occasionally survive in Middle English, e.g., "As
sende love and pees betwixe hem two" (desire/command),
but obviously the history of the English subjunctive is one
of simplification, ultimately to the vanishing point.

Only a single Old English verb, *hātan* (call/command)
discloses a formal passive *voice*. In addition to the strong
preterit *hēt*, which is active and transitive, the verb has a
weak preterit, *hātte*, used for both present and past as a
passive: "Rachel *hātte* Iacobes wif" (Jacob's wife was called
Rachel). Like modern German, Old English frequently
employs the impersonal (*man* plus verb) in lieu of the
passive; but the language also offers an abundance of
phrases built on *bēon/wesan/weorþan* plus past participle:
wæs hāten, wæs nemned, wearþ ofslægen, wæs ahafen. A
passive infinitive concept was rendered with the active,
e.g., hēht him *lǣran* (ordered him to learn, or to be taught).

One further aspect of the verb may be noted as of
interest. The Old English will sometimes imply a verb
phrase through context, where only the auxiliary and not
the infinitive is stated. Thus, in "þā hīe þā dūne gesāwon,
þǣr þǣr hīe tō scoldon tō ofslēanne Isaāc" (when they saw

the hill, where they should [go] to slay Isaac), the concept *go/proceed* must be inferred. Students of Elizabethan English will readily recall the comparable usage here: "I must away, I'll to London."

III

Finally, the early role of the preposition calls for comment. We are accustomed to regard the prepositional phrase as a modifying unit, but originally the preposition functioned as possibly more than a connective. The Old English offers the familiar prepositional phrase patterns (*on* his wīngeard, *intō* mīnum berne, *æfter* fēawum dagum, *tō* mīnum fæder, *uppan* ānre dūne, *betwix* Īotum and Seaxum), but also shows modifications of the pattern that suggest an adverbial role for the preposition itself. Frequently it follows pronouns (þūs cweþende him *tō*, cwæþ him þūs *tō*) in such a way as to suggest itself as a separable verb prefix, in the manner of modern German (*anfangen*, *zuhören*), modifying the sense of the verb. And certain of the Old English adverbs of place, þǣrtō, þǣrintō, hērinne, may be considered as reversed prepositional phrases, with the first part of the compound standing as an indefinite pronoun concept: to *that place*, into *that place*, in *this place*. Our modern legal language, with its fondness for such compounds, is actually offering us an ancient kind of syntactic shorthand.

Appendix

THE PRODIGAL SON
St. *Luke Gospel*, XV: 11-32

Old English

Hē cwæþ: Sōþlīce sum man hæfde twegen suna. Þā cwæþ sē gingra tō his fæder: "Fæder, sele mē mīnne dǣl mīnre ǣhte, þe mē tō gebyreþ." Þā dǣlde hē him his ǣhta. Þā ǣfter fēawum dagum eall his þing gegaderode sē gingra sunu, and fērde wrǣclīce on feorlen rīce, and forspilde þǣr his ǣhta, libbende on his gǣlsan. Þā hē hīe hæfde ealle āmierrede, þā wearþ micel hungor on þǣm rīce and hē wearþ wǣdla. Þā fērde hē and folgode ānum burgsittendum men þæs rīces; þā sende hē hine tō his tūne þæt hē hēolde his swīn. Þā gewilnode hē his wambe gefyllan of þǣm bēancoddum þe þā swīn ǣton; and him man ne sealde. Þā beþōhte hē hine and cwæþ: "Ēalā, hū fela hȳrlinga on mīnes fæder hūse hlāf genōhne habbaþ, and ic hēr on hungre forweorþe.

Ic ārīse, and ic fare tō mīnum fæder, and ic secge him: 'Ēalā, fæder, ic syngode on heofonas and beforan þē; nū ic neom wyrþe þæt ic bēo þīn sunu nemned; dō mē swā ānne of þīnum hȳrlingum.' " And hē ārās þā and cōm tō his fæder. And þā gīet þā hē wæs feorr, his fæder hē hine geseah, and wearþ mid mildheortnesse āstyred, and ongēan hine arn, and hine beclypte and cyste hine. Þā cwæþ his sunu: "Fæder, ic syngode on heofon and beforan þē; nū ic ne eom wyrþe þæt ic þīn sunu bēo genemned." Þā cwæþ sē fæder tō his þēowum: "Bringaþ raþe þone sēlestan gegyrelan and scrȳdaþ hine; and sellaþ him hring on his hand and gescȳ tō his fōtum; and bringaþ ān fætt styric and ofslēaþ: and uton etan and gewistfullian; forþǣm þes mīn sunu wæs dēad, and hē geedcucode; hē forwearþ, and hē is gemēt." Þā ongunnon hīe gewistlǣcan. Sōþlīce his ieldra sunu wæs on æcere, and hē cōm. And þā hē þǣm hūse genēalǣhte hē hīerde þone swēg and þæt werod. Þā clipode hē ānne þēow and ascode hine hwæt þæt wǣre. Þa cwæþ hē: "þīn broþor cōm; and þīn fæder ofslōh ān fæt cealf for þǣm þe hē hine hālne onfēng." Þā bealg hē hine and nolde in gān; þā ēode his fæder ūt and ongan hine biddan. Þā cwæþ hē his fæder andswarigende: "Efne swā fela gēara ic þē þēowode, and ic nǣfre þīn bebod ne forgīemde; and ne sealdest þū me nǣfre ān ticcen þæt ic mid mīnum frēondum gewistfullode. Ac siþþan þes þīn sunu cōm, þe his spēde mid miltestrum āmierde, þū ofslōge him fætt cealf." Þa cwæþ hē "Sunu þū eart simble mid mē, and ealle mīne þing sint þīne. Þē gebyrede gewistfullian and blissian for þǣm þes þīn brōþor wæs dēad and hē geedcucode. Hē forwearþ and hē is gemēt."

[Tenth Century]

Middle English

And he seide, A man hadde twei sones; and the gonger of hem seide to the fadir, Fadir, gyue me the porcioun of catel, that fallith to me. And he departide to hem the catel. And not aftir many daies, whanne alle thingis weren gederid togider, the gonger sone wente forth in pilgrymage in to a fer cuntre; and there he wastide hise goodis in lyuynge lecherously. And aftir that he hadde endid alle thingis, a strong hungre was maad in that cuntre, and he began to haue nede. And he wente, and droug hym to oon of the citeseyns of that cuntre. And he sente hym in to his toun, to fede swyn. And he coueitide to fille his wombe of the coddis that the hoggis eeten, and no man gaf hym. And he turnede agen to hym silf, and seide, Hou many hirid men in my fadir hous han plente of looues; and Y perische here thoroug hungir. Y schal rise vp, and go to my fadir, and Y schal seie to hym, Fadir, Y haue synned in to heuene, and bifor thee; and now Y am not worthi to be clepid thi sone, make me as oon of thin hirid men. And he roos vp, and cam to his fadir. And whanne he was git afer, his fadir saig hym, and was stirred bi mercy. And he ran, and fel on his necke, and kisside hym. And the sone seide to hym, Fadir, I haue synned in to heuene, and bifor thee; and now Y am not worthi to be clepid thi sone. And the fadir seide to hise seruauntis, Swithe brynge ge forth the firste stoole, and clothe ge hym, and gyue ge a ryng in his hoond, and schoon on hise feet; and brynge ge a fat calf, and sle ge, and ete we, and make we feeste. For this my sone was deed, and hath lyued agen; he perischid, and is foundun. And alle men bigunnen to ete. But his eldere sone was in the feeld; and whanne he cam, and neigede to the hous, he herde a symfonye and a croude. And he clepide oon of the seruauntis, and axide, what these thingis weren. And he seide to hym, Thi brother is comun, and thi fadir slewe a fat calf, for he resseyuede hum saaf. And he was wrooth, and wolde not come in. Therfor his fadir wente out, and bigan to preye hym. And he answerde to his fadir, and seide, Lo! so many geeris Y serue thee, and Y neuer brak thi comaundement; and thou neuer gaf to me a kidde, that Y with my freendis schulde haue ete. But aftir that this thi sone, that hath deuourid his substaunce with horis, cam, thou hast slayn to hym a fat calf. And he seide to hym, Sone, thou art euer more with me, and alle my thingis ben thine. But it bihofte for to make feeste, and to haue ioye; for this thi brother was deed, and lyuede agen; he perischide, and is foundun.

[*Fourteenth Century*]

Early Modern English

He said moreouer, A certaine man had two sonnes. And the yonger of them sayde to his father, "Father, giue me the portion of the goods that falleth to mee." So he deuided vnto them his substance.

So not long after, when the yonger soone had gathered all together, hee tooke his iourney into a farre countrey, and there hee wasted his goods with riotous liuing. Nowe when hee had spent all, there arose a great dearth throughout that land, and he began to be in necessitie. Then he went and claue to a citizen of that countrey, and he sent him to his farme, to feede swine. And hee woulde faine haue filled his bellie with the huskes that the swine ate: but no man gaue them him.

Then hee came to himselfe, and sayd, "Howe many hyred seruants of my fathers haue bread ynough, and I die for hunger? I will rise, and goe to my father, and say vnto him, 'Father, I haue sinned against heauen, and before thee. And am no more worthie to be called thy sonne: make me as one of thy hyred seruants.'"

So hee arose, and came to his father, and when hee was yet a great way off, his father sawe him, and had compassion, and ranne and fell on his necke, and kissed him. And the sonne sayde vnto him, "Father, I haue sinned against heauen, and before thee, and am no more worthy to be called thy sonne."

Then the father said to his seruants, "Bring forth the best robe, and put it on him, and put a ring on his hand, and shooes on his feete, and bring the fat calfe, and kill him, and let vs eate and be mery. For this my sonne was dead, and is aliue againe: and hee was lost, but hee is found." And they began to be mery.

Nowe the elder brother was in the fielde, and when hee came and drewe neere to the house, hee heard melodie, and daucing, and called one of his seruants, and asked what those things meant. And hee said vnto him, "Thy brother is come, and thy father hath killed the fatted calfe, because hee hath receiued him safe and sound." Then he was angrie, and would not goe in: therefore came his father out and intreated him. But hee answered and sayd to his father, "Loe, these many yeeres haue I done thee seruice, neither brake I at any time thy commaundement, and yet thou neuer gauest me a kid that I might make merie with my friends. But when this thy sonne was come, which hath deuoured thy goods with harlots, thou hast for his sake killed the fat calfe."

And he said vnto him, "Sonne, thou art euer with mee, and all that I haue is thine. It was meete that wee should make merie and be glad: for this thy brother was dead, and is aliue againe: and hee was lost, but he is found."

[*1560*]

Suggestions for Further Reading

Baugh, Albert. *A History of the English Language*. 2nd ed. New York: Appleton-Century-Crofts, 1957.

Brook, G. L. *A History of the English Language*. New York: W. W. Norton, 1964.

Campbell, A. *Old English Grammar*. Oxford: Clarendon Press, 1959.

Frey, Leonard H. *Readings in Early English Language History*. New York: Odyssey Press, 1966.

Jesperson, Otto. *Growth and Structure of the English Language*. Garden City, N.Y.: Doubleday Anchor Books, 1955.

Mossé, Fernand. *A Handbook of Middle English*. Tr. by James A. Walker. Baltimore: Johns Hopkins Press, 1952.

Myers, L. M. *The Roots of Modern English*. Boston: Little, Brown, 1966.

Pyles, Thomas. *The Origins and Development of the English Language*. New York: Harcourt, Brace, and World, 1964.

Quirk, R., and Wrenn, C. *An Old English Grammar*. Rev. ed. New York: Holt, Rinehart and Winston, 1957.

Wright, J., and Wright, E. M. *An Elementary Middle English Grammar*. 2nd ed. London: Oxford University Press, 1928, 1957.